INCREDIBLE YOU

Rhys Brisenden

ILLUSTRATED BY Nathan Reed

TATE

Now and again (and I do this too)
You might want to be someone
other than you.

Perhaps at the end
of a very **BAD** day

You might wish you were a **BIRD** and could just fly away?

Or maybe you think being a **DOG** looks like fun?

You could chase squirrels up trees

or dig holes in the sun.

And, if you ever felt angry,
you could shout in the park
Because, if you were a dog,
it would just sound like a

BARK!

Perhaps you'd rather be a **CAT**, after all, if sometimes you like to curl up in a **BALL?**

You'd get behind-the-ear scratches
and rubs on your belly,
While you lay on the sofa and watched **CARTOONS** on telly.

Now, the remarkable thing about being a **FISH**
Is that you get to eat all the seaweed
you wish.

And, while you might never have given seaweed a try,

To a fish it's delicious, like **BLUEBERRY PIE.**

Or what about animals
that live in the zoo?

There **MUST** be an animal
there that suits you!

Tigers are
FIERCE, giraffes
are so
TALL,

A panda, perhaps?

A mountain gorilla?

A short-tailed, or long-tailed, fluffy

chinchilla?

A hippo? A lizard? A lion? Ah, I know!

You **MUST** want to have

the strength of a

RHINO!

ROAR!

Now, I know what you're thinking:
that all sounds pretty good
And you'd still like to be
someone else if you could.

But you're

TRULY AMAZING

Think of the things you can do!

Perhaps you'll realise if I name just a **FEW?**

You can do funny voices

that make people GIGGLE.

You can write a kind note,

then sign your name with a *squiggle*

You can make up a **STORY** or read from a **BOOK.** You can **SMELL,**

you can **TASTE**, you can **LISTEN** and **LOOK**.

You can draw with your **HANDS**

and score goals with your **FEET.**

Or **MAKE UP** your own rules!

You can **SING!**
If anyone says
you can't
they are
wrong!

You just
keep singing your
own special song.

And I bet you can
touch
your **NOSE**
with your
TOE.

And, if
not, don't worry.
At least now you know!

You can

SLEEP . . .

Just let

yourself drift away

And **DREAM** of the things you

hope will happen one day.

And, when you wake up,
you can make them come true!

I'm not joking. You can!
And yes, I mean YOU!

You're fab and fantastic!
You're one of a kind.
You're unique
and **AMAZING**.
Always bear that in mind.

So there's only one thing that I'd like you to do

And that's **NEVER** stop wanting to be

For my boys, Charlie and Sam ...
stay incredible xx – N.R.

For my mum, who taught me
how incredible books can be – R.B.

First published 2019 by order of the Tate Trustees
by Tate Publishing, a division of Tate Enterprises Ltd,
Millbank, London SW1P 4RG

www.tate.org.uk/publishing
Text © Rhys Brisenden 2019
Artwork © Nathan Reed 2019

First published 2019

ISBN 978 1 84976 626 5

Distributed in the United States and Canada by ABRAMS, New York
Library of Congress Control Number applied for
Printed and bound in Printed and bound in China by C&C Offset Printing Co., Ltd
Colour Reproduction by Colour reproduction by Evergreen Colour Management Ltd